DAVE RAMSEY

THOMAS NELSON
Since 1798

NASHVILLE DALLAS MEXICO CITY RIO DE JANEIRO BEIJING

Published in Nashville, Tennessee, by Thomas Nelson. Thomas Nelson is a trademark of Thomas Nelson, Inc.

Thomas Nelson, Inc. titles may be purchased in bulk for educational, business, fund-raising, or sales promotional use. For information, please e-mail SpecialMarkets@ThomasNelson.com.

Scripture quotations marked (KJV) are taken from the *Holy Bible,* King James Version, Cambridge, 1769.

Selections from *The Holy Bible, New King James Version* (NKJV) ©1982 by Thomas Nelson, Inc. Used by permission. All rights reserved.

The scripture quotations herein designated (NRSV) are from the New Revised Standard Version Bible, © 1989 by the Division of Christian Education of the National Council of the Churches of Christ in the U.S.A. Used by permission. All rights reserved.

Scripture quotations marked (NIV) are taken from the HOLY BIBLE, NEW INTERNATIONAL VERSION®. NIV®. ©1973, 1978, 1984 by International Bible Society. Used by permission of Zondervan. All rights reserved.

Library of Congress Cataloging-in-Publication data on file
with the Library of Congress.

ISBN 10: 1-4041-0461-5
ISBN 13: 978-1-4041-0461-7

Printed in the United States of America

07 08 09 10 11 RRD 5 4 3

"There is ultimately only one way to financial peace, and that is to walk daily with the Prince of Peace, Christ Jesus."

Why Journal?

I want to talk you into doing something you normally wouldn't do. I want you to track your progress through your Total Money Makeover in writing. Journaling this process in detail will be a huge tool and great treasure for you if you make the effort. I know that writing everything down as you go means more work, but the payoff will be well worth it.

Take this journal and record everything happening that seems like a big deal. Record the relationship issues, the debt, the emotions, the setbacks, the victories, and anything else that seems important at the time. Just so you know: I am not a big journaling nerd. But I did this through my process of going broke and losing everything. While you are heading the other direction with your Total Money Makeover, you will likely get the same benefits I got by journaling.

The immediate benefits of writing everything down are twofold. First, writing helps you process the problems and victories. Have you ever had a problem and sat down with a friend for advice? We have all had the experience that by the time we finished describing the problem, we knew the answer. The reason that we answered our own question is that in order to verbalize the problem we converted our jumbled thoughts to concise ideas that clarified the situation. The same thing happens when you write out the "crisis of the day" or—hopefully more often than not—your latest victory. This new clarity will help you move faster through your Total Money Makeover.

The second immediate benefit of journaling is that you can reread your entry just days—even months—later and gain vital perspective on your progress. When we were going broke, I remember entering a very emotional, hopeless entry. It was right after we lost one of our apartment complexes to foreclosure. "Gloom, despair and agony on me. . . ." It sounded like a *Hee Haw* song. My entry pretty much revealed how I knew life on the planet was over thanks to this particular foreclosure. Of course, it wasn't. The weird thing is that just a few weeks later, while still heading toward bankruptcy, I reread my entry and laughed. Rereading my hopeless entry didn't depress me; it gave me perspective. I realized that life on the planet hadn't ended, so maybe—just maybe—I was being a little melodramatic. This isn't to devalue the feelings I had in the middle of the crisis, but to highlight the fact that the next time I faced a "planet ending crisis" I was better prepared, emotionally and spiritually. Journaling helps you see the big picture during your Total Money Makeover.

But I think possibly the best reason to do this journal is that it makes a generational gift. I have a copy of my great great grandfather's memoirs. He fought in the Civil War, later founded a college, and even later became a preacher. The memoirs are full of challenges, humor, and wonderful stories. If you leave this book full of what you experience while having your Total Money Makeover to your great great grandchildren, you will have left a real treasure.

I believe that if you do with money what we teach, then you will literally be able to financially change your family tree. I think it would be very cool to leave this journal to document how you did it. So here is my challenge:

Write it down.

You will be glad you did.

—DAVE RAMSEY

"For which of you, intending to build a tower, does not sit down first and count the cost, whether he has enough to finish it . . ."

LUKE 14:28–30 (NKJV)

"If you want things you have never had, you have to do things you have never done."

"You can't spend your way out of guilt."

"Money can be the light that exposes wounds or other problems in the midst of a volatile setting."

"How you handle or mishandle your money tells
us who you are, and, more important,
it tells *you* who you are."

"The understanding that the wealth is really God's
and you are managing it not only for yourself,
but also for the good of others frees you."

"The earth is the LORD'S, and the fulness thereof . . . "

PSALM 24:1 (KJV)

"Do the things that are important in ways
that are noble and you will be led to
More Than Enough."

"Saving and investing with vision makes you rich.
This is one of the reasons the rich get richer."

"Vision that is rooted in values
is the only vision that will last."

"Goals are the practical building blocks
that make a vision come true."

"Goals make the difference."

"Courage always gets you dirty;
you have to be in the middle of the action
to create action."

"When money is in your possession what you do
with it screams loudly who you are."

"Problems give us the ability to hang on
and that ability changes who we are."

"[S]orrow looks back, worry looks around,
while faith looks up."
—ANONYMOUS

"Hope is stolen when we misunderstand failure."

"Don't allow failure to steal your hope."

"It isn't just how we spend money;
it's also how we handle our finances
that mark us as opposites."

"The past can hurt, but you can either run from it or learn from it."
—RAFIKI IN *THE LION KING*

"The power of being connected to people pulling the same way adds insight, ingenuity, ideas, values, energy and good habits that can mushroom."

"Criticize a man in financial difficulty and you
will see instant and dramatic flight or fight."

"We know in our minds that staying in the pit isn't smart, but it is our pit and it feels safe."

"When life ties you up and throws you in a pit you have to make choices. You have to decide what to do at the bottom."

"You must have power to be truly gentle."

"Cowards can never be moral."
—MAHATMA GANDHI

"The most powerful form of behavior modification
is the properly run small group."

"Intensity is a key ingredient in the lives
of people who win."

"Some folks have their feet planted firmly on the
ground and move like it. Other folks
understand or at least have a glimpse
of the power of momentum."

"[T]he bulk of the blame [for this credit excess] lies with the character represented in our financial institutions and their decision makers."

"Concentration: put all your eggs in one basket
and watch that basket."
—DALE CARNEGIE

"Prayer is vital, but God is not in the business
of rewarding the lazy."

"If you spend your day looking for easy work,
you will still go to bed worn out."

—ANONYMOUS

"Do not be conformed to this world, but be transformed by the renewing of your mind."

ROMANS 12:2 (NKJV)

"The habits, character traits, and abilities that make someone able to build wealth also make him able to manage it."

"Those who have never made a mistake usually work for those who have."
—HENRY FORD

"You cannot have healthy relationships and build
wealth with lies as your foundation."

"I have never been poor, only broke.
Being poor is a frame of mind."
—MIKE TODD

"The problem with the clenched-fist
money-management style is that while those
dollars can't get away, new dollars
can't get in, either."

"Nature gave us two ends—one to sit on and one
to think with. Ever since then man's success
or failure has been dependent on which
one he used most."
—GEORGE KIRKPATRICK

"No discipline seems pleasant at the time, but painful. Later on, however, it produces a harvest of righteousness and peace for those who have been trained by it."

HEBREWS 12:11 (NIV)

"The more mature you are the longer you can wait
for the satisfaction that completion brings."

"When you learn to respect others, adults and children, you will see yourself improve in self-esteem, happiness, and fulfillment."
—SHARON RAMSEY

"Far and away the best prize that life offers is the chance to work hard at work worth doing."
—TEDDY ROOSEVELT

"When you give, passion, joy, and intensity come
to you like waves crashing at the seashore."

"I do not know anyone who has gotten
to the top without hard work."
—MARGARET THATCHER

"If you give because you think that makes God owe you a favor and you are promised to get more, you will mess up the whole process."

"[M]oney is just the method that the Great Teacher
has chosen to expose and correct our flaws as well
as give us 'attaboys' for a job well done."

"Vision that has no foundation and depth in values
is merely a dream, and you will
wake up disappointed."

"I have found that the best way to handle money properly is to trick yourself into it."

"Do not attempt to do a thing unless you are sure
of yourself; but do not relinquish it simply
because someone else is not sure of you."
—STEWART WHITE

"If a man hasn't discovered something that he
will die for, he isn't fit to live."
—DR. MARTIN LUTHER KING, JR.

"Who can find a virtuous wife? For her worth is far above rubies. The heart of her husband safely trusts her; So he will have no lack of gain."

PROVERBS 31:10–11 (NKJV)

"There can be no money secrets from someone you are serious enough about to marry."

"I'm a great believer in luck, and the harder
I work the more I have of it."
—THOMAS JEFFERSON

"Hope is the powerful fuel that causes the engine
of your life to develop all the horsepower
it was designed to have."

"There is an old Danish proverb that says if you give a child everything he wants when he cries and a pig everything he wants when he grunts you will have a fine pig and a sorry child."

". . . [T]he most important decision in achieving a
goal is not what you are willing to do to achieve it,
but what you are willing to give up to achieve it."
—EARL NIGHTINGALE

"One big hairy lie that we allow to steal our hope
is [this]: Failure is permanent."

"Failure is natural, normal, and is going to happen."

"Not all the wealthy are wise, but usually the wise
will become wealthy given time."

"Marriage doesn't mean you lose your identity or competence, it does mean you have brought someone into your life you would die for. You have to die alright, die to self."

"Quiet strength is to wear power lightly,
understanding that power is just like money—
it is only a tool to help others."

"It is much better to look where you are going
than to see where you have been."

"Meekness is not weakness,
it is power under control."
—WARREN WIERSBE

"... [H]ope is the core of what makes people become what God designed them to be."

"When hope is gone we quit."

"In an age when all our answers and information come in sound bites, we have lost an understanding of working through a process. And even more critically, we have lost the understanding of what true wisdom is."

"Courage seems to be something that is not talked about any more."

"Men feel better solving problems, while ladies
feel better by talking about problems."
—JOHN GRAY

"Even though talking might be hard . . .
communication will save your marriage."

"Giving works because it is your personal
blueprint to be a giver . . ."

"Failure is the opportunity to begin again
more intelligently."
—HENRY FORD

"[C]hildren have never been very good at listening
to their elders, but they have never failed
to imitate them."
—JAMES BALDWIN

"If we take all the lessons learned from failure
and stack them [up] we can easily get the
breathtaking view that hope gives."

"Your compass is your values; they lead you to the road, which is vision, and you are able to find your way using the road signs, called goals."

"When money problems hit the scene we also take that as a direct indication of personal failure."

"Deception equals destruction."

"In a culture that seems to give respect to loud
mouths, we seem to have labeled those
with quiet strength as weak."

"Men and women are limited not by their
intelligence, nor by their education, nor by the
color of their skin, but by the size of their hope."
—JOHN JOHNSON

"Bring all the tithes into the storehouse, That there may be food in My house, And try Me now in this," Says the Lord of hosts, "If I will not open for you the windows of heaven And pour out for you such blessing that there will not be room enough to receive it."

MALACHI 3:10 (NKJV)

"Diligence . . . comes with a guarantee."

"Prosperity may be a bigger test than poverty
when it comes to exposing your weaknesses."

"Hope placed properly is one of the most powerful forces you will ever know."

"Remember, hope is on your side as long
as you keep it there."
—SHARON RAMSEY

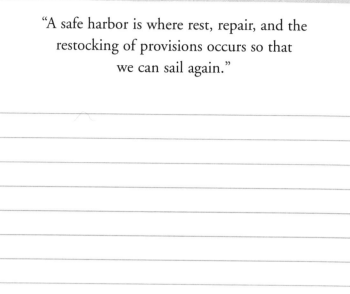

"A safe harbor is where rest, repair, and the restocking of provisions occurs so that we can sail again."

"And we know that all things work together for good to those who love God, to those who are the called according to His purpose."

ROMANS 8:28 (NKJV)

"If you want uncommon results you have to think and do things that are uncommon."

"There are no hopeless situations, only people
who are hopeless about them."
—DINAH SHORE

"When a man refuses to act like a man, his wife
will act like his mother."
—ED COLE

"Man must cease attributing his problems to his environment, and learn again to exercise his will, his personal responsibility."
—ALBERT SCHWEITZER

"The trouble with most of us is that we would
rather be ruined by praise than saved by criticism."
—NORMAN VINCENT PEALE

"Personal finance is 80 percent behavior
and only 20 percent head knowledge."

"The quality of a person's life is in direct proportion
to their commitment to excellence, regardless of
their chosen field of endeavor."
—VINCE LOMBARDI

"When times are good and you are on a mountaintop in your life you need to maximize your life and your wealth."

"Intensity is a decision to attack, to have passion, and to purposefully put power into your thoughts and actions."

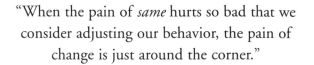

"When the pain of *same* hurts so bad that we consider adjusting our behavior, the pain of change is just around the corner."

_____

_____

_____

_____

_____

_____

_____

_____

_____

_____

_____

_____

_____

_____

_____

_____

_____

_____

_____

_____

_____

_____

"Those people who you are with for life are the
ones who naturally lend themselves to holding
you accountable and are the ones
who will support you."

"[Real courage] is courage that reflects values
and stands firmly on them."

"The first requirement of success is the ability to apply your physical and mental energies to one problem incessantly without growing weary."
—THOMAS EDISON

"When you have contentment you can easily get out of debt."

"People change their lives when they say
'I've had it!'"
—LES BROWN

"[I]t is worth the trouble to become the person
you know God made you to be."

"People who don't give are stopped up.
Things flow in but nothing flows out."

"Where there is no vision, the people perish."

PROVERBS 29:18 (KJV)

"One of the most important gifts you can teach
your children is the power of initiative.
Move on it! Go get it!"

"Backward momentum is as powerful and
hard to stop as forward momentum."

"God asked Solomon what he wanted and
the answer was wisdom."

"Money is a mirror that, strange as it sounds,
reflects our personal strengths and weaknesses
with amazing clarity."

"Ninety percent of investing is just doing it."

"The pressure and drama that are created by silence born of patience will make you money in negotiations."

*"In the house of the wise are stores of choice food and oil,
but a foolish man devours all he has."*
PROVERBS 21:20 (NIV)

"A get-rich-quick mentality has at its core a laziness."

"You aren't anyone else's job."

"Hard work claims very few victims."

"Hard work opens locked doors."

"If you measure success in service,
money will flow to you."

"When one door closes, another opens;
but we often look so long and so regretfully upon
the closed door that we do not see the one
which has opened for us."
—ALEXANDER GRAHAM BELL

"Our culture worships information, but information without application is an empty deity."
—DENNIS RAINEY

"The rich rule over the poor, and the borrower is the slave of the lender."

PROVERBS 22:7 (NRSV)

"If you want to have more joy and more wealth than most people do you have to live more excellently than they do."

"Work keeps us from three evils:
boredom, vice, and poverty."
—VOLTAIRE

"Hope is the fuel that when ignited turns you, the rocket, loose with intensity, and all the while accountability is your guidance system that will keep you between the ditches."

"If you don't like the way something is,
do something about it."

"You don't have time or brain power to worry
when you are focused on work."

"God answers all prayers.
His answer can be yes, or no, or grow."
—CHUCK SWINDOLL

"Values matter because having principles you live by brings you joy, peace, and yes, even wealth."

"The plans of the diligent lead surely to plenty, But those of everyone who is hasty, surely to poverty."

PROVERBS 21:5 (NKJV)

"Discipline understands that the best way
to get rich quick is to get rich slow."

"There is no excuse to retire broke
in America today!"

"Discipline is the middle name of the wealthy."

"The thing that moves or motivates us is . . .
disturbance or dissonance."

"Teaching your children to work is one of the best gifts a loving parent can give."

"There is a power and patience to discipline."

"[TV sets] are stealing our quality time.
They are not evil and you can tell by my familiarity
that they are in our home; but we are not afraid
to turn them off—nor should you be."

"The best time to plant an oak tree is twenty
years ago, the next best time is now."
—DAVID CHILTON

"Finger-pointing, blame shifting, and whining,
while they appear to have merit,
are not doing something."

"There is also real delight when you get to earn money with the sweat of your brow and then use that money to help others by giving."

"[W]hen it comes to the people we love,
love is spelled *T-I-M-E.*"
—GARY SMALLEY

"The difference between a successful person and others is not a lack of strength, not a lack of knowledge, but rather a lack of will."
—VINCE LOMBARDI

"You'll never leave where you are,
until you decide where you'd rather be."
—LEWIS DUNNINGTON

"Teaching your children to work is also a way of building a meaningful relationship with them, one that will last for years and years—and long beyond the 'injustice' of having to do chores."

"By removing work from a child's life you cripple him."

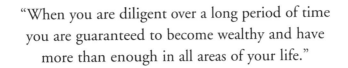

"When you are diligent over a long period of time you are guaranteed to become wealthy and have more than enough in all areas of your life."

"Real power is gentle, not boastful or rowdy like a
teenager in a car with a big engine. . . .
[It is] becoming what God intended you to be."

"Patience that is the fruit of endurance gives you
an increased ability to respond to life,
rather than react to it."

"He with the most toys when he dies is dead."

—BUMPER STICKER

"In our macho, hyper culture, we've mistaken contentment for weakness, rather than seeing it for what it really is: born of strength."

"When bad stuff happens, resist the human urge
to blame and instead join the
elite group called the doers."

"Work is doing it. Discipline is doing it every day.
Diligence is doing it well every day."

"A valid attempt that fails is different from a life full of get-rich-quick schemes that didn't work."

"Courage born of wisdom is powerful courage,
not just simply bravery,
but deeply held real courage."

"When someone recognizes a way to get more pleasure or avoid pain they are moved, motivated, in that direction."

"If we are desperate enough,
sometimes we think shortcuts are okay."

"Desperation gives you the heart of a cheater."

"A good man leaves an inheritance to his children's children, But the wealth of the sinner is stored up for the righteous."

PROVERBS 13:22 (NKJV)

"You have more than enough only
when you give it away."

"Patience born of maturity will make you rich.
It will make you rich in dollars
and rich in relationships."

"There is no question that quality time is what is needed to develop strong fruitful relationships."

"Contentment is found in character, not circumstances that are made better with money."

"Contentment can be gathered again when we learn to slow down and count life's simple pleasures."

"Without courage,
all other virtues lose their meaning."
—SIR WINSTON CHURCHILL

"When you teach diligence to children you are teaching them to have vision and to think long term."

"Use the joy and peace you receive from your blessings to give you the energy and motivation to tackle your worries."

"The heart of someone . . . who thinks
get-rich-schemes will work for them
is the heart of a cheater."

"You find [contentment] by learning from your situation and fighting through it to make your character change and learning to win wherever you are."

"And not only that, but we also glory in tribulations, knowing that tribulation produces perseverance; and perseverance, character; and character, hope. Now hope does not disappoint, because the love of God has been poured out in our hearts by the Holy Spirit who was given to us."

ROMANS 5:3–5 (NKJV)

"Giving is an amazing process because it violates common sense, which tells us if we let go we will have less, not more."

"You can't shake hands with a clenched fist."
—GOLDA MEIER

"We all know that wealth is not a way to tell for sure that someone is wise, but we have all made the mistake of thinking that wealth is more important than wisdom."

"Surplus wealth is a sacred trust which its possessor
is bound to administer in his lifetime for the
good of the community."
—ANDREW CARNEGIE

"A faithful man will abound with blessings, But he who hastens to be rich will not go unpunished."
PROVERBS 28:20 (NKJV)

"You are made in God's image and He is a giver; so that means in order for you to be all you can be you must be a giver too."

"When you give of yourself you can't help but
be lifted up and energized to fight
your own problems."

"After twenty years of studying millionaires across a wide spectrum of industries, we have concluded that the character of the business owner is more important in predicting his level of wealth than the classification of his business."
—DR. THOMAS J. STANLEY

"The people who are the happiest and the wealthiest got that way by giving."

"We have exchanged the old layaway pay-until-paid plan for a new credit card 'lay-awake' plan."

"Hate is not the opposite of love, apathy is."

"Patience knows that one definition of maturity
is learning to delay pleasure."

"When you give expecting, you are selfish,
and that does not bring you more money
or better relationships."

"If the two of you [spouses] aren't in harmony with your money, you aren't really in harmony at all."

"Patience allows you to keep your wealth because it makes you decide what something is worth to you."

"No one would remember the Good Samaritan if he only had good intentions. He had money as well."
—MARGARET THATCHER

"Life is an exciting business, and most exciting
when it is lived for others."
—HELEN KELLER

"We are so marketed to that we have started to believe that more stuff will make us happy. But in this country, more stuff has resulted in more debt."

"Connection, strong connection,
takes time and lots of being very real."

"The fun thing is that when you start to hit some new levels of contentment and peace you will be catapulted into yet even higher levels."

"Contentment is not apathy and yet
we often confuse the two."

"Contentment is only born of strength."

"[B]usiness is like tennis:
Those who serve well win."
—KEN BLANCHARD

"Giving shows strength, perspective, maturity,
and a noble selflessness that has become rare."

"Giving works because you are designed
to be a giving being."

"Patience is having the nobility to wait because the result is more important than personal pleasure."

"All you can do is all you can do,
and that is enough."
—ART WILLIAMS

"We used to be a country that admired diligence, thrift and integrity. What we must remember is that money allows us the leverage to do good."

"Integrity matters."

> *"In quietness and in confidence shall be your strength."*
> ISAIAH 30:15 (KJV)

"I don't know what your destiny will be, but one thing I know; the only ones among you who will be really happy are those who will have sought and found how to serve."

—ALBERT SCHWEITZER

"Intensity that will not be denied is the
mother of initiative."

"If you don't like where you are, you have to
change what you have been doing.
And that takes intensity."

"Never fear that the fire can be too hot because [God] has his hand on the thermostat."

"Over the long term you get what you deserve, and none of us like it when what we deserve is pain."

*"Give portions to seven, yes to eight, for you do not know
what disaster may come upon the land."*

ECCLESIASTES 11:2 (NIV)

"The happiest and most joyful people are those
who give money and serve. . . .
We serve and give our way into true joy."

"Those with the most power in the patience category seem to endure with the most class and with the most ease."

"There is no shortcut to any place
that is worth going."
—BEVERLY SILLS

"Marketing has entered our homes and
has stolen our peace."

"You must pay the price if you want to
secure the blessing."
—ANDREW JACKSON

"Being powerful is like being a lady. If you have
to tell people you are, you aren't."
—MARGARET THATCHER

"You will seldom meet someone with patience rooted in power who has not seen heavy trials."

"Contentment is more than things, or stuff;
it's your ability to cope with and deal with
your situation and circumstances."
—SHARON RAMSEY

"Teaching your children how to use their money responsibly means teaching them to *save.*"

"*Blessed is the man who finds wisdom, the man who gains understanding.*"

—PROVERBS 3:13 (NIV)

"Work like it all depends on you and
pray like it all depends on God."
—St. Ambrose

"I can do all things through Christ who strengthens me."

PHILIPPIANS 4:13 (NKJV)

"The depth and commitment of your relationship must match or be deeper than the seriousness of the problem being confronted."